WITHDRAWN

Published in 2012 by The Rosen Publishing Group, Inc.
29 East 21st Street, New York, NY 10010

Library of Congress Cataloging-in-Publication Data

Campbell, Carol P.
Frequently asked questions about teen pregnancy / Carol
P. Campbell, Tamra Orr.—1st ed.
    p. cm.—(FAQ: teen life)
Includes bibliographical references and index.
ISBN 978-1-4488-4627-6 (library binding)
1. Teenage mothers—Juvenile literature. 2. Teenage
pregnancy—Juvenile literature. I. Orr, Tamra. II. Title.
HQ759.4.C36 2012
306.874'3—dc22

2010045922

Manufactured in the United States of America

CPSIA Compliance Information: Batch #S11YA: For further information, contact Rosen Publishing, New York, New York,
at 1-800-237-9932.

Contents

WHAT ARE SOME FACTS ABOUT TEEN PREGNANCY?

Pregnancy, whether accidental or not, is a complicated, emotional event for the pregnant woman, her partner, and those close to her. Raising a child is a huge commitment that requires enormous amounts of time, effort, and money. For teenagers, pregnancy presents particularly challenging obstacles. At a time when most other people their age are still dependent on their parents for money, food, and shelter, pregnant teens are suddenly faced with adult responsibilities. They must consider the changes a baby will bring, including the ways it will affect their plans for school, a career, and relationships.

According to the National Campaign to Prevent Teen Pregnancy, more than 820,000 teenage girls become pregnant every year in the United States. By the age of eighteen,

A teacher explains birth control methods in a sex education class at a Kansas high school. Teen pregnancy rates are high in the United States because of young people's lack of understanding about reproduction and contraception.

one out of every three girls will have been pregnant at least once. Eighty-two percent of pregnant teens say that they never expected to become pregnant. One of the reasons for the high rate of teen pregnancy is that many teens do not have enough informa-tion about sex, birth control, and how their reproductive systems function. Often they are afraid or embarrassed to ask questions. The first step in preventing unwanted pregnancies is to understand how your body works.

Physical and Emotional Changes: Puberty

When you reach the age of eleven or twelve, your body starts to change. You may feel some of these changes, but you might not be able to see their effects right away. This time of physical and emotional change is called puberty. During puberty your glands begin to produce hormones—chemicals that make you look and feel different. Hormones are responsible for most of the physical and emotional changes typical of puberty. For boys, hormones lead to the production of sperm, the deepening of the voice, and the growth of facial hair. For girls, breast development and the beginning of menstruation are some of the changes that occur during puberty.

The Human Reproductive Systems

The male reproductive system, like the female reproductive system, consists of those organs that help produce offspring. The male body produces sperm, which swim in a thick, cloudy white liquid. This combination of liquid and sperm is called semen. When a man becomes aroused, his penis fills with blood and becomes erect (hard and straight). If he is fully stimulated, he has an orgasm and ejaculates (releases) semen. The average ejaculation contains five hundred million sperm—only one of which is needed to make a woman pregnant.

Semen usually leaves the male body during ejaculation, but it is possible for some to leak out of the erect penis even without an orgasm. Pregnancy can occur without intercourse if semen comes near the vaginal area and sperm manage to enter the vagina and swim up into the uterus. While this is unlikely,

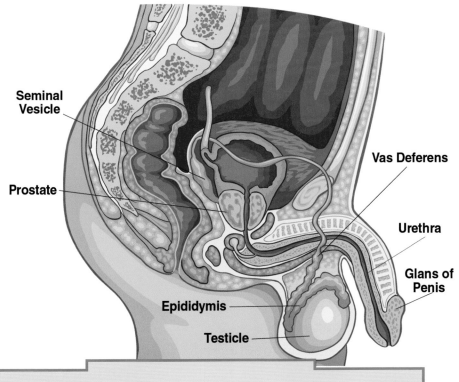

Seminal Vesicle

Prostate

Vas Deferens

Urethra

Glans of Penis

Epididymis

Testicle

The male reproductive organs are located inside and outside the pelvis. They include the testicles, the duct system of the epididymis and vas deferens, glands (including seminal vesicles and prostate), and the penis.

it is possible. Because the penis releases a small amount of sperm-containing pre-ejaculatory fluid before orgasm, a woman can also become pregnant even if the penis is pulled out of the vagina before climax. That's why if you decide to have sex, it is important to use some form of birth control, preferably a condom in conjunction with another form, from the first moment of sexual contact.

The condom is a rubber sheath that covers the penis and creates a barrier between it and the vagina. Condoms prevent semen from leaking into the vagina. They protect against pregnancy as well as sexually transmitted diseases (STDs) such as acquired immunodeficiency syndrome (AIDS). Other than abstinence, condoms, when used properly, offer the best protection against pregnancy and disease of all forms of birth control. While the birth control pill offers better protection against pregnancy, it does nothing to prevent STD infection.

Traditionally, condoms have been made from latex. But you may have seen newer polyurethane condoms, too. Some people claim that polyurethane condoms are more sensitive than latex ones because they are thinner in texture. But studies show that polyurethane condoms are not as effective in protecting against pregnancy and sexually transmitted diseases. Polyurethane condoms are more likely to slip off the penis during withdrawal and also to break. The bottom line is, unless you are among the small number of people allergic to latex, latex condoms are a far safer option.

In the female reproductive system, a woman's organs are involved in producing ova, or eggs. A woman is born with a certain number of ova. These are stored in her two ovaries. During puberty the menstrual cycle begins, and these eggs begin to mature. Each month, one egg is released from the ovary. This process is called ovulation. The egg then travels through one of the two fallopian tubes located on either side of the uterus. If the egg is not met by a sperm, the unfertilized egg will break down. Each month, the lining of the uterus thickens in preparation for

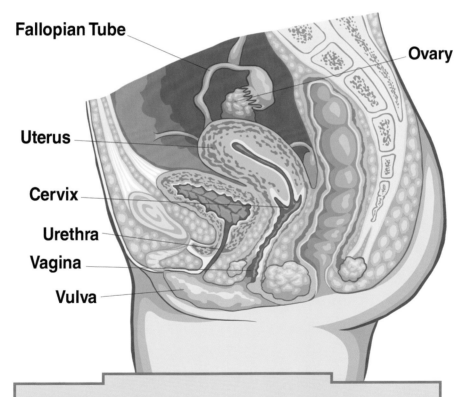

Fallopian Tube

Ovary

Uterus

Cervix

Urethra

Vagina

Vulva

The female reproductive system includes the vulva, vagina, cervix, uterus, fallopian tubes, and ovaries. The vagina is the canal where menstrual fluid comes out during a period and where a baby would come out during childbirth.

carrying a baby. If the egg is not fertilized, the lining is pushed out of the body along with the unfertilized egg. This is called menstruation (the monthly period).

However, if sperm should enter the woman's body while the egg is in the fallopian tube, a single sperm can fertilize the egg. This is known as the moment of conception. The fertilized egg then drops into the uterus. If it successfully implants itself in the wall of the uterus, the egg will begin to grow and develop. The woman is now pregnant. If all goes well during pregnancy, a baby will be born about nine months later.

WHAT IF YOU
ARE PREGNANT?

You've just found out that you're pregnant. You're probably in a state of shock and disbelief. You may be frustrated, panicked, scared, or even angry. Your emotions are probably mixed; you might be sad, terrified, disappointed, and even a little curious and hopeful all at once. You may be wondering how you can even begin to make the important life decisions that pregnancy demands when your emotions are so mixed up. You need to begin prenatal care as soon as you determine you are pregnant.

Pregnancy means thinking about many different things at once. Some of those things may be completely new and strange. You will have to think about how your body will change and how you will care—or if you can care—for a helpless infant on your own. Pregnancy also means you will have a lot more responsibility in your life. You need to think about what is best for you, the baby, the baby's father, and your family.

Getting Information

Every decision requires that you find out the facts about your situation. The more you know, the better your decision will be. To make a good, informed decision about being pregnant, you should know or learn the answers to most of these questions:

1. What happens to my body when I am pregnant?
2. What do I need to do while I am pregnant to prepare for the baby's arrival?
3. How and where do I learn how to care for a baby?
4. What does it cost to have a baby?
5. How mature am I? Can I handle being a mother?
6. Is adoption an option, and if so, is it something I feel comfortable doing?
7. Is abortion an option, and if so, is it something I feel comfortable doing?
8. Who are the people I can talk to without fear or embarrassment? Where can I get objective information and advice about all of these things?
9. How will I go to school once the baby is born?

Facts and guidance about teen pregnancy are usually easy to find. They can be just a phone call away. If you feel comfortable talking to your parents about pregnancy, they may be the best people to speak to. At school, you may have a special relationship with a teacher, guidance counselor, or school nurse. Or perhaps there is a favorite aunt or uncle or old family friend that you trust. One of these people can be a good source of advice and information.

Facing Your Feelings

Getting the facts about pregnancy will probably fill you with even more questions. Those questions will help you to confront and explore your feelings. Thinking about your feelings and coming to an understanding of what you believe and what you

These teens speak to their high school guidance counselor about personal issues and feelings. Sometimes it helps to talk to people you can count on or who have experienced pregnancy and who can offer direction and answers to your questions.

really want will help you make good decisions. Here are some questions that you may want to ask yourself:

1. Am I upset and confused? Am I too worried to see the situation clearly? Who can help me feel less troubled?
2. Do I feel alone? Whom can I trust enough to talk to? Whose advice do I trust the most?
3. Am I hoping that pregnancy will solve some of my problems or cure my unhappiness? Do I think that having a baby will fix a relationship with the baby's father? Am I hoping that having a baby will finally give me somebody to love and care for and who will love and care for me?
4. Am I thinking about the other people involved? Have I considered the role my family and the father of my child will play once the baby is born?
5. Am I thinking about my feelings/hopes/wants for the future? Am I thinking about what will be best for me AND for the baby?

It is never wise to make a decision when you are afraid or unsure. Decisions made in fear or without sufficient knowledge have a greater risk of turning out to be mistakes. Facing your feelings and knowing all the facts are critical steps on the path toward making important decisions.

Issues to Think About

A pregnant teenager has many questions, concerns, fears, uncertainties, and conflicting emotions. Considering these issues should help clarify the situation a little and calm you, and make you feel more in control. Thinking about the following issues will help you begin the decision-making process and encourage you to begin taking the appropriate actions to support your decision:

- **Your age and maturity.** Sometimes there are health risks for a girl who is pregnant at a young age. These risks may affect the mother or the baby. Sometimes there are risks for both the mother and the baby. A doctor should be asked about these risks. You also need to think

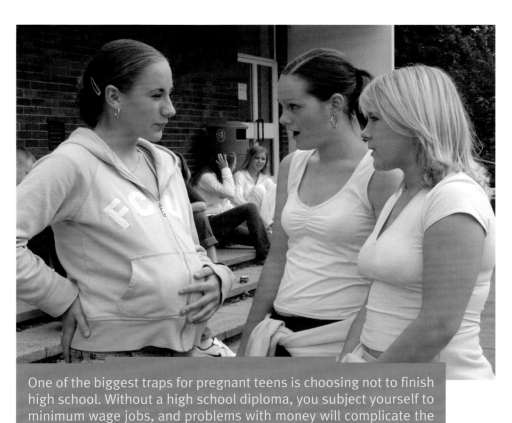

One of the biggest traps for pregnant teens is choosing not to finish high school. Without a high school diploma, you subject yourself to minimum wage jobs, and problems with money will complicate the challenges of parenthood.

carefully about how the baby will affect your life. Do you feel ready to accept the responsibility of pregnancy? Will you be able to care for the baby once it is born and when it grows up? How will you feel if you have to stay home on the weekends to take care of your baby while all your friends are out having a good time?

- **Graduating from school.** You must think about how the baby will affect your ability to finish school. Raising a baby requires time and money. You need a good education to find a job that pays enough to take care of a baby. These days, even graduating from high school is not enough education for many jobs. Many teens attend college after high school. Will you be able to do this? Who will take care of your baby while you're at school? Can you afford to hire someone to look after your baby? Are your parents willing to help out? Will you be able to go to school and work at the same time?

- **The role of the father.** You must think about the father. He is the other person who is most affected by the situation. If you know who the father is, you must find out if he will help. Will he help you with money? Will he help you with emotional support? Will he be a good father? Is he mature and responsible? Can you raise a baby without him? You may not know for sure who the father is. Sometimes you do know, but he has gone away. Sometimes he is just "out of the picture." Are you willing to let your baby grow up without a father? Can you make it on your own?

- **Place of residence.** A baby must have a home. Maybe it can be with your family or with the father's family. Maybe you can live on your own. Maybe you and your child can live with friends. You must figure out how the home will function. If you live with others, who will be in charge? Whose rules will the baby follow? Can the new home support a baby?

- **Finances.** A pregnant teen must also think about money. Having a baby is expensive. Medical costs are very high. You must pay for food and clothing. Other costly items are needed, such as baby supplies. Are you old enough to get a job? Would you be able to keep the job after the baby is born? How soon after the birth would you be able to go back to work? Even if you can get a job, it may not pay enough to support both you and the baby. And you might need to pay for a babysitter or a day care center to take care of your child while you are at work.

- **Your relatives.** Support from your family is very important. Can your family or the baby's father's family offer you any help? Remember that help doesn't have to be in the form of money or a place to live. Parents, siblings, and other relatives can offer you vital emotional support, too, not to mention babysitting help. If your family does not support you, emotionally or financially, how will this affect your baby's life and your life should you choose to have the baby?

- **Giving up your baby.** What are your feelings about adoption? Do you feel you could give up your baby for

Many pregnant teens might be anxious that the news of their pregnancy will make their parents fly into a rage. Parents might respond badly at first, but that doesn't mean that they won't eventually stand by you and encourage you.

adoption and be able to get past the sadness and move on with your life? Do you feel other people could offer your child a better life and more opportunities?

- **Your physical condition.** It is critical to think about your health and identify any health problems that may make your pregnancy dangerous or difficult. Both mothers and fathers should think about health conditions, such as diseases, that can affect the fetus (developing baby).

Some diseases are hereditary, and they can be passed on to the baby through genes from both the mother and the father. If either parent carries the genes for a hereditary disease, there is a chance that the baby will be born with the disease.

STDs, which are most commonly spread through bodily fluids during sex, can also be passed from a mother to her baby. Some kinds of STDs can be passed on to the fetus though the mother's blood while the fetus develops in her uterus. Other kinds can be passed from the mother to the baby during delivery. Some of the most common STDs include syphilis, gonorrhea, genital herpes, and AIDS. STDs can have a variety of harmful effects on the baby, including low birth weight and birth defects. Some can even cause premature birth.

- **Drugs, alcohol, and cigarettes.** Taking drugs can also hurt your unborn child. Illegal drugs such as marijuana, cocaine, crack, uppers, downers, LSD, and heroin can be very harmful to a fetus. So can legal drugs, including nicotine and alcohol, over-the-counter medicines, and many prescription drugs.

Alcohol consumption can result in miscarriage, birth defects, low birth weight, and a condition called fetal alcohol syndrome, which results in mental and physical impairments and is the leading cause of mental retardation in the Western world. Cigarettes contain nicotine, a dangerous drug. Smoking can harm both you and the fetus. It causes veins and arteries to become smaller. That means that the heart has to work harder to pump blood to the rest of the body. Babies whose mothers smoke usually weigh less and are weaker at birth than other babies. Smoking also makes it harder for you to breathe. Smoking can make the risk of miscarriage four times more likely, and if a pregnant woman smokes more than twenty cigarettes each day, the risk is six times greater. Recent studies have even proved that nonsmoking pregnant women who live with a smoker and inhale secondhand smoke can increase their risk of miscarriage.

Drugs can be dangerous not only to the mother but also to the fetus. This is because drugs are easily passed from mother to baby through the blood. If the mother is using drugs while she is pregnant, her baby may be born addicted. Illegal drugs bought on the street include marijuana, heroin, amphetamines (uppers), barbiturates (downers), cocaine, and crack. Legal drugs prescribed by a doctor or bought over the counter can be just as dangerous as street drugs. Aspirin, cough syrups, diet pills, acne medications, nose drops or sprays, laxatives, and vitamin supplements can be harmful in some cases, so be sure to check with your doctor before using them. Whatever you eat, the fetus eats. Whatever you drink or smoke, the fetus does, too. Remembering this can make it easier to stick to healthy habits during pregnancy. Make sure to tell your doctor about your drug history; he or she will then decide if your baby is at risk.

- **Looking ahead.** A baby changes its parents' plans for the future. What are some things you may not be able to do once your child is born? Do you plan to finish high school? Go to college? Have a professional career? Can you do those things with a baby? Perhaps you can find a teen mom that chose to have her baby and ask her about how she dealt with these questions and how her life has been since having the baby.

Your answers to some of these questions should help you clarify and organize your thoughts and help you begin to evaluate what is best for you, your unborn baby, and the child's father so you can plan a course of action and make the necessary preparations.

The Father's Viewpoint

You've just found out that your girlfriend is pregnant. You're probably feeling panicked and scared and very confused about what the right thing to do is. The first and most important thing to do is be there for your girlfriend. If you think you're scared, imagine how she feels. Talk to her, comfort each other, express your fears, and try to help calm each other.

The next step is to begin an honest and realistic discussion of your options. First, ask yourself what you feel is the best way to approach this situation. Do you and your girlfriend want to stay together? Do you feel ready to be married? Do you think you are both ready and able to raise a child? What are your feel-

Family planning clinics can provide the opportunity to talk with nurses and counselors about options for having the baby, adoption, or abortion. Many family planning clinics will link new parents to financial resources if they decide to keep the baby.

ings about adoption or abortion? After thinking about these things on your own, share your thoughts with your girlfriend, and listen carefully to her ideas. It would be great if you both came to an agreement about what to do, but remember, ultimately this will be her decision to make. You should respect her decision, even if you disagree with it. And if she does decide to keep the baby, you should be prepared to offer financial and emotional help and your time throughout the child's life, even if you and the mother do not stay together. The child is your responsibility, too, and you must do your part to ensure he or she is well provided for.

three

WHAT DO YOU NEED TO KNOW DURING YOUR PREGNANCY?

Many women experience physical discomfort during pregnancy. They are rarely serious medical problems, and a good relationship with a doctor will help manage your discomfort and worries. It is crucial that you see a doctor and get prenatal care. And if you ever feel something is seriously wrong, call 911 or go to a hospital immediately.

Nausea

Most women experience morning sickness. Nausea and vomiting typically occur in the morning but can also happen throughout the day. Morning sickness generally occurs in the first twelve weeks of pregnancy and then goes away. It is not usually serious. It will not endanger the health of the mother or baby, as long as you make sure to get enough nutrients when you aren't feeling

Most women experience morning sickness when they are in their first twelve weeks of pregnancy. It is good to drink water and eat several small meals throughout the day to help control morning sickness and to keep you and the baby healthy.

nauseated and stay hydrated. Although there is nothing you can take to stop morning sickness, there are things you can do to feel more comfortable. Some women find that their nausea is worse if their stomachs are empty. It is a good idea to eat several small meals each day to keep something in your stomach at all times. If the smell of a certain type of food makes you nauseated, try to avoid it. If you vomit often, drink lots of water and other non-caffeinated, unsweetened liquids to replenish the lost fluid. You don't want to become dehydrated; dehydration can have serious effects for you and the baby. When you're dehydrated you lose electrolytes—substances such as sodium and potassium—that help your body and its organs function properly.

Unpleasant Burning Sensation in the Chest and Other Discomforts

Another common problem associated with pregnancy is heartburn, a form of indigestion. It occurs in about half of all pregnant women. Heartburn is a burning sensation in the middle of the chest accompanied by a sour taste in the mouth. Heartburn is caused by stomach acid in the esophagus. The muscle that seals the stomach from the esophagus is weakened. As a result, the stomach acid flows into the esophagus. Heartburn tends to get worse as the pregnancy progresses. This is because your stomach is moved out of place by your growing uterus. Pregnant women can avoid heartburn by eating smaller, more frequent meals to let the food soak up all the acid in the stomach. They should also eat slowly and avoid greasy foods.

Other common problems during pregnancy include back-ache, constipation, hemorrhoids, and sleeping problems. Some of these problems may seem like causes for concern, but they are normal in almost every pregnancy. You may not experience all or any of these problems.

Pregnancy Stages

A typical pregnancy, from the time the egg is fertilized until the birth of the baby, takes about nine months. The pregnancy is divided into three trimesters, which are each three months long.

- **First trimester.** It is during the first trimester that the embryo (the baby during the first two months of its life) develops the major organs. During the beginning of this period, the head, legs, and arms begin to grow and develop. By the eighth week, the embryo's face appears, as do the fingers and toes. It is also at this point that it begins to develop sexual organs.

    At the end of the first trimester, the embryo is considered a fetus. Instead of a cluster of cells, the fetus resembles a baby. The heart starts to beat. At this point, the fetus is about 3 inches (7.6 centimeters) long and weighs about 1 ounce (28.4 grams).
- **Second trimester.** During the second trimester, the fetus begins to grow larger. The organs that developed during the first trimester begin to mature. At this point, a doctor is able to determine the sex of the baby. The

fetus begins to grow eyebrows and eyelashes as well as hair on the head. The fetus can move around a bit. The fetus weighs about 1 pound (453.6 g) and measures about 12 inches (30.5 cm) long.

Many women consider their second trimester to be the easiest part of a pregnancy. This is because the mother feels less nauseated, and the fetus is still not big enough to prevent her from comfortably going about her daily activities.

- **Third trimester.** This is the period when pregnant women gain the most weight. The average baby grows

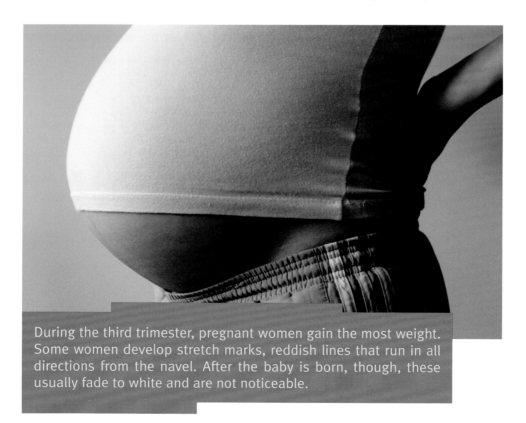

During the third trimester, pregnant women gain the most weight. Some women develop stretch marks, reddish lines that run in all directions from the navel. After the baby is born, though, these usually fade to white and are not noticeable.

from about 1 pound (453.6 g) to about 7.5 pounds (3.4 kilograms) during the third trimester. At the end of this trimester, the baby is ready to be born.

Changes in Your Emotions and Body

Pregnancy causes many emotional and physical changes. Hormonal changes may cause you to be moody while you are pregnant. This is normal. Let friends and family know that you may sometimes act differently during your pregnancy. They can help you to cope during this time. Guidance counselors, doctors, friends, and family members all want to help you have a smooth, trouble-free pregnancy and a healthy baby if you choose to become a teen mother.

Taking Care of Yourself

If you are pregnant, your most important job is taking care of yourself. That is especially true for a teenager. A teenager's own body is still growing and developing, and therefore has special requirements.

It is important for pregnant women to stay healthy by eating right. Not only will they feel better, but their babies will be more likely to be born healthy and have a good birth weight. The growing fetus gets its nutrients directly from the mother.

Because they are still growing and developing, pregnant teenagers should be especially careful about their diets. Pregnant teens must be sure to eat well-balanced meals rich in vitamins and minerals to provide enough nutrients for both themselves and their babies.

Pregnancy is not the time to go on a diet. In fact, pregnant women should expect to gain a considerable amount of weight. The usual amount of weight gain is anywhere from 25 to 40 pounds (about 11 to 18 kg), depending on the mother's needs, body type, experience with morning sickness and nausea, and metabolism. She should consult with a doctor about what sort of nutrition goals and body weight will be healthiest for her.

The key is to increase your food intake in a nutritious, healthy way. You are eating for two now, and your caloric intake must increase as a result. Select more foods from the milk and dairy groups for extra calcium, and be sure to get lots of protein from meats, poultry, fish, eggs, and nuts. Plenty of fresh fruit and vegetables will provide essential vitamins. It is also important to drink lots of fluids, especially water. Try drinking milk or juice instead of soda. Avoid fast foods, snack foods, and candy, which are high in fat, sugar, and cholesterol and relatively low in nutrients.

Physical Activity and Special Conditioning

Exercise is very important to a healthy pregnancy. It can relieve stress, build strength, and make for a quicker recovery. But choosing the right kind of exercise is crucial. It is not a good idea to begin a strenuous exercise program while you are pregnant. Jerky, bouncy exercises should be avoided, especially after the first few months. Contact sports, racquetball, skiing, and bicycle riding are also not safe for pregnant women.

However, low-impact exercises such as walking, swimming, stationary bike riding, and special aerobics classes for pregnant women are all safe ways of exercising during pregnancy. Still, it is important to consult a doctor about your exercise plan.

Many pregnant women practice special exercises that are designed to make pregnancy and delivery go more smoothly. These exercises focus on strengthening the lower back, stomach, and leg muscles, which are the areas that suffer the most strain during pregnancy and childbirth. Learning good posture

These moms-to-be practice some yoga moves during a Lamaze class. Exercises can increase body strength and ease mental and emotional stress. Learning breathing control will aid a pregnant teen during childbirth.

and safe ways to bend and lift objects can also help cut down on muscle strain. A good resource may be your local fitness center or YMCA where prenatal yoga classes are offered.

Exercise classes are also offered specifically for pregnant women and teens. One of the most popular of these is Lamaze. Lamaze classes, which teach special breathing exercises to make delivery easier, are for the mother-to-be and a partner who will be present during labor. The partner may be the baby's father, a friend, or a relative.

It is important for both your physical and mental well-being to get back into shape after your baby is born and continue to eat well. Good health will allow you to better meet the challenges of motherhood.

Getting Enough Rest

A big part of staying fit is getting plenty of rest. A pregnant woman may feel especially tired during the first trimester. She may need to take naps. As a result, finding time for school and friends can be difficult. Teens who work may have to change or even cut their hours to make sure that they get enough rest.

Getting Regular Checkups for You and Your Baby

First, you should see a doctor. The doctor will give you a complete examination. You can also get information on pregnancy care at the doctor's office. A doctor who takes care of pregnant

A midwife discusses health care with a pregnant teen. Midwives practice in a range of settings: private practices, doctors' offices, health maintenance organizations (HMOs), hospitals, health departments, or birthing centers.

women and delivers babies is called an obstetrician. Some pregnant women prefer to use a midwife—a woman who is not necessarily a doctor or registered nurse but who is qualified, trained, and certified to deliver babies. Most midwives prefer natural birthing methods that avoid painkilling drugs and surgery if at all possible. There are many different ways to find an obstetrician or a midwife. Most family doctors can recommend an obstetrician. Hospitals also have obstetricians or midwives they can recommend. Some midwives work at special birthing centers or clinics.

You should have regular checkups throughout your pregnancy. The doctor will need to know when your last normal period began. This will help him or her to figure out when you became pregnant and when you are due to deliver. The doctor will also perform an examination. The exam will reveal the size of your uterus. This helps to tell how far along the pregnancy is.

The doctor may use a test called a sonogram. A sonogram uses sound waves to take a picture of the fetus. Sometimes doctors use sonograms later in the pregnancy. They help detect problems as the fetus grows.

It is important to tell the doctor about any drugs you have taken—including over-the-counter, illegal, or prescription drugs—since you became pregnant. Ask the doctor if it's OK to take medication before you take any, even aspirin. You may decide to breast-feed your baby. Then you will need to be careful about medicines even after the baby is born. Medicines will be passed to the baby in your milk. You should also avoid

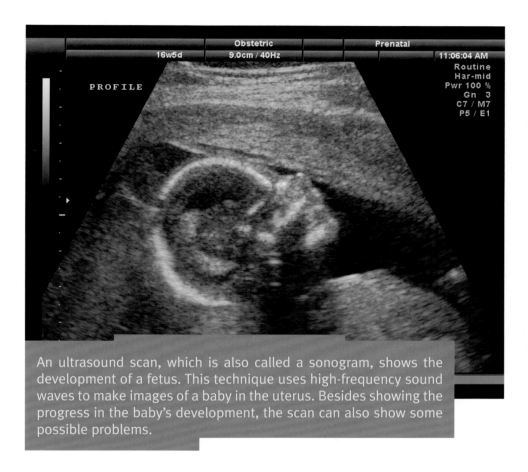

An ultrasound scan, which is also called a sonogram, shows the development of a fetus. This technique uses high-frequency sound waves to make images of a baby in the uterus. Besides showing the progress in the baby's development, the scan can also show some possible problems.

having X-rays during pregnancy. X-rays can upset the normal growth of a fetus.

Some Medical Risks for Pregnant Teens

As a teenager, you have special risks during your pregnancy. You are more likely to give birth to a premature baby. Premature babies are born earlier than the full nine months. These babies are more likely to have birth defects. They also have a greater chance of getting infections after birth. You run the risk of getting toxemia and anemia. Toxemia causes high blood pressure and makes the hands and feet swell. Anemia is a deficiency in red blood cells, which makes you tired and weak. The doctor should take blood tests and urine tests. Your blood pressure should be checked often. Remember, a healthy mother means a healthy baby.

Ten Great Questions to Ask Your Doctor

1. What is the most effective type of birth control, and how do I use it?

2. How do I know when I am ovulating? How do I monitor my menstrual cycle?

3. What do I do if I get pregnant? What resources are available to me?

4. What legal responsibility do I have if I get a girl pregnant?

5 How does the adoption system work for single teens?

6 What should I know about having a baby?

7 How are abortions done? How much do they cost? Where do I get one?

8 What are the symptoms of STDs? What are the treatments? How will my baby be affected by my STD?

9 If I give my baby up for adoption, will I ever get to see him/her again?

10 How do I tell my parents if I am pregnant/my girlfriend is pregnant?

four

WHAT IF YOU DECIDE NOT TO KEEP OR HAVE THE BABY?

While some teens who become pregnant decide that keeping the baby is the right decision for them, other teens come to a different conclusion. If you decide that you don't want to have or care for your baby, you should be aware of your options. Adoption and abortion are two choices to think about.

Giving Up the Baby

Adoption is the process in which a pregnant woman gives birth and then turns her baby over to an adoption agency. She gives up all of her legal rights to the child. After a careful screening process, the agency chooses a parent or parents who will raise the baby as their own. Sometimes the adoption process is done privately, however, and begins before the mother has given birth. The birth mother can help choose a couple or person

A mother feeds her adopted daughter. In most cases, if you decide to put your baby up for adoption at an agency, you will have nothing to do with your child once he or she has been handed over to an adoptive couple.

that she feels comfortable turning her baby over to after she or he is born.

Agencies often place babies with married couples who can't have children of their own. Increasingly, same-sex couples and single people are adopting children, too. Some single parents wish to raise the child alone; others intend to eventually establish a lifelong relationship with a partner who will coparent.

Adoption laws can vary greatly from state to state. This is especially true of laws determining how much information about birth parents can be released to adoptees (adopted people). In nearly all states, adoption records are sealed until the adoption is finalized. In some states, adoption records remain sealed, meaning that adoptees will never gain access to information about their birth parents. Most states, however, now allow adoptees over the age of eighteen to receive nonidentifying information about their biological (birth) parents, if requested in writing. This means that an adoptee can find out some information about his or her parents, such as when and where the adoption took place, and the parents' ages, physical description, race, ethnicity, religion, education level, and important medical information—everything except their actual names. A few states release identifying information, including names, to adoptees who have turned either eighteen or twenty-one.

Adoption Agencies and Arrangements

If you are considering adoption, you should contact an adoption agency. Even better, try to speak with representatives from many different agencies. Each has its own rules and procedures.

A good agency will provide a counselor for you to speak with about adoption. He or she will talk to you about your options, your reasons for considering adoption, and your rights and responsibilities. An agency should never make you feel that you must go through with the adoption. Putting a child up for adoption is a very hard decision to make and requires time and thought. No one should ever try to rush you. If you change your mind before the adoption is finalized, your decision should be respected without argument.

Deciding whether to give up a child for adoption is probably one of the most difficult choices to make. You may change your mind many times during pregnancy. You don't have to be certain of your decision until you are ready to sign the legal papers. A good agency will wait until the baby is born to ask the mother to sign an official agreement.

Agencies are usually very careful about selecting adoptive parents. Interested couples or individuals must prove to the agency that they will be good parents and can provide a good home in both a material and emotional sense. Representatives from the agency visit the homes of individuals or couples to see how they live and find out how much money they earn. They also request letters from people who know the candidates. In the letters, friends or coworkers express what they think about the person's or couple's ability to be good parents.

If you are not participating in a private adoption, in which the adoption arrangements are made with you and the adoptive parents before the baby is born, you may never know who the adoptive parents are. Likewise, the adopting parents may never find out who you are. This is known as closed adoption. Some agencies are now advocating open adoptions, in which the birth and adoptive parents meet, exchange contact information, and maybe even form a lifelong relationship, in which the birth parents have contact with the child. It must be remembered, however, that the adoptive parents are that child's parents. Open adoptions do not give you any parenting rights. The adoptive parents decide how much or how little contact they want between you and the child.

After Adoption Papers Are Signed

After the adoption agreement is signed, the baby is given a new birth certificate. It is then the duty of the adoptive parents to name the child. After the adoptive parent or parents take the baby home, there may be a waiting period. It can last as long as six months to a year. Until then the adoption is not final. A worker from the agency visits the child's new home during this time to see how the baby and the parent or parents are doing. The worker makes sure that the baby is being treated properly. The adoption is final after this waiting period. The legal papers are then sealed, and the mother cannot get the child back.

Independent Adoptions

In some cases, it is possible to set up an independent adoption, also called private adoption, in which a pregnant teen is matched with a person or couple who is interested in adopting a child. These are usually arranged with the help of a family doctor or a community member such as a priest or a rabbi. A lawyer is called on to draw up an agreement. The adoptive couple usually pays some of the mother's expenses, which can include medical costs, living expenses, and lawyer's fees.

Private adoptions are different from agency adoptions. They often are not as strict. Adoptive parents may be friends of the pregnant teen's family or friends of friends. The adopting parents are not as carefully selected and do not undergo the tests required by most agencies. In addition, decisions about identifying information of the birth parent or ongoing relationships between the birth and adoptive families must be worked out between the two parties.

Selecting the Appropriate Agency

Can your agency be trusted? It is very important to find out. There are ways to check on an agency. Try to keep the following things in mind when identifying an adoption agency:

- Look for sound advice.
- Request to see the agency's official papers and proof of certification. These should include certificates and licenses that show that the agency is allowed to operate in a given state.
- Inquire about how long the agency has been in business. If it has been around for a long time, it is probably trustworthy.

- Get recommendations. If you have any friends or family members who have either adopted or given a baby up for adoption, ask them about their experiences with an agency and if they would recommend it.
- Follow your intuition and that of your family. If the agency does not seem like it will be supportive in putting your baby up for adoption, choose another agency.

Putting a baby up for adoption is always a very difficult decision. But for many pregnant teens, it is the best thing to do.

Ending a Pregnancy

Abortion is the termination, or ending, of a pregnancy. In most cases, the pregnancy can be ended by a simple procedure in a doctor's office or clinic.

Having an abortion can be an intensely emotional experience and is a very hard topic to discuss for many people. While a majority of Americans feel that abortion should be legal in the United States, a very large number of people believe that abortion is morally wrong and violates their religious beliefs. Some people think that abortion is OK only if it is done early in a pregnancy. Others say that abortion should be allowed until later in the pregnancy. Still others feel it is never right to have an abortion, even in cases of rape or problem pregnancies in which the mother's health and life are endangered. And, like any major medical procedure, abortion has risks. No matter what other people think, you must decide for yourself how you feel about abortion and whether it is an option for you.

Here are some important facts to consider about abortion:

- As is true of any surgical procedure, abortions pose some health risks, but they are basically safe if performed by a doctor. Risk increases as the pregnancy advances.
- Abortions can be performed in a doctor's office or in a clinic. It is very important to make sure that a doctor performs the procedure. Illegal abortions are very dangerous and can lead to life-threatening infections or loss of blood.
- There are many different methods of abortion. The method used depends on how advanced the pregnancy is.
- If performed correctly, abortions are not usually physically painful, though some people experience minor discomfort after certain procedures.

Court Rulings and Abortion

Abortion has been legal in the United States since 1973. Since then, there have been thirty abortion-related court rulings. Abortions during the three stages of pregnancy are limited in varying degrees, depending on the state where the procedure will be performed. During the first three months of pregnancy, abortions are legal in all U.S. states. Some states restrict second-trimester (third to sixth month) abortions, and some prohibit abortion altogether during the third trimester (sixth to ninth month).

As with adoption laws, there are some laws regarding abortion that specifically affect teens. As of late 2010, according to the Guttmacher Institute, thirty-four states require some parental involvement in the decision of a minor (under the age of eighteen) to have an abortion. Planned Parenthood will be able to advise you on the laws in your state.

Get Counseling

You should get counseling before you decide on an abortion. A good abortion clinic will provide trained counselors who make sure that patients who are considering abortion know all the important facts and carefully weigh the pros and cons of the decision. To receive confidential counseling, contact Planned Parenthood or another organization.

Your Well-being

It is vital to find a safe place to have an abortion. When done properly, most procedures are not dangerous. If abortions are not performed correctly, however, serious problems can result. The best place to go is to your doctor. If he or she can't perform the procedure, ask your doctor for names of other health professionals who can help you. You can also obtain listings of doctors and clinics from school and community counselors. Some agencies such as Planned Parenthood offer free information and counseling to teens.

Safe Haven Laws

Sometimes teens decide against abortion, have their baby, and then immediately regret their decision and panic about what to

Members of a teen youth group in New Jersey hang posters outlining the Safe Haven Protection Act. Since the act became law, mothers can leave their newborns at a local hospital or police station without having legal action taken against them.

do next. Don't worry; help is out there. Almost all U.S. states have a Safe Haven law to help protect newborn babies from abandonment. These laws offer options for parents who feel unable to care for their new baby.

Safe Haven laws allow the baby's parents to drop off the child at a Safe Haven location anonymously and without fear of being arrested for abandonment or neglect. Safe Haven locations include hospitals, emergency medical services, police stations, and fire stations. The Safe Haven location may request your name and family history, but they will not force you to share information if you don't want to.

It's important to note that, if you drop off your baby at a Safe Haven location, you are officially giving up custody of the baby. Also, you cannot simply leave the baby at the Safe Haven location, assuming that someone will find him or her. You have to physically hand the baby to someone at the Safe Haven location.

The specifics of the law vary from state to state. Many states accept children who are one month or younger, but the age ranges from younger than one year to younger than seventy-two hours. Some states require that a parent drop off the baby, while others let the parent designate someone else to do the drop-off.

Myths and Facts

Myth

Learning about contraception and birth control will tend to make teens more sexually active and increase the risk of pregnancy. Fact: ➡ Research has shown just the opposite. Two studies published in 2005 indicate that laws limiting teenagers' access to birth control and information about contraception fail to reduce sexual activity and actually increase the risk of unplanned pregnancy and STDs. The first study, published in the *Journal of the American Medical Association*, found that one in five teenagers would have unsafe sex if their parents had to be notified when they got birth control at a family planning clinic. The second study, published in *Perspectives on Sexual and Reproductive Health*, discovered that the more teens knew about birth control and the more positive their attitudes about it, the more likely they were to use it and the less likely to become pregnant.

 More than half of teen pregnancies happen during the first six months after a girl has sex for the first time. Fact: ➥ Half of teen pregnancies occur in the first six months of sexual activity and 20 percent occur within the first month of a girl's first experience with sexual intercourse.

 A girl cannot get pregnant while she is having her period. Fact: ➥ Sperm can survive inside of you for up to a week and can fertilize an egg when your period is over.

five

WHAT DO YOU NEED FOR A NEWBORN?

If you decide to keep your baby, there are many things you should prepare for before birth. These concern both the baby's health and well-being and your own.

Preparations

Once you decide to raise your child, you will have even more choices to make. Your baby will need a crib to sleep in for the first couple of years. The crib will need sheets, blankets, and liners. You will also need baby supplies such as soaps, creams, powders, lotions, nipples, and bottles. You may be able to have a baby shower, in which your friends and family give you some of the basics that you will need in the first weeks and months. You may also check with your school counselor, local church, or community mental health center for information on financial supplements for

A newborn will need many accessories, including bathing supplies. Always check with the Consumer Product Safety Commission (http://www.cpsc.gov) before buying baby cribs and other supplies to make sure you are purchasing items that have not been found to be harmful to children.

first-time mothers, or programs, such as the Women, Infants, and Children (WIC) Program, for low-income mothers. These supplements can help you purchase some of the necessities as well as provide you with helpful resources to obtain information.

Your baby will need clothes as it grows and diapers for the first few years. You may get clothes for the first few months at your baby shower, if you have one. You can also ask for hand-me-downs from older friends or sisters who have had children. Secondhand stores sell inexpensive but quality baby and child clothes. You will have to choose between cloth and disposable diapers. Cloth diapers are cheaper and more environmentally friendly, but they are a bit more trouble. Cloth diapers must be washed and dried every time your baby is changed, though it is possible to sign up with a cloth diaper delivery service that drops off clean diapers and picks up your dirty ones for laundering. Disposables are very convenient, but they are more expensive. Plastic diapers also create a great deal of trash, which is not good for the environment.

Breast-feeding (also called nursing) and bottle-feeding have their own pros and cons. The American Academy of Pediatrics recommends that women who don't have health issues should try to breast-feed their babies for at least the first six months of the newborn's life.

You will also have to choose how you want to feed your baby. There are basically two choices: breast-feeding and bottle-feeding. Over the years, pediatricians have gone back and forth over which method is better. Each has its own advantages and its own disadvantages. Breast-feeding is free and requires no cans, bottles, or preparation. It is also thought to be healthier for the baby, leading to the development of a stronger immune system among other benefits. But breast-feeding can be done only by the mother (unless she pumps breast milk and stores it for later use in bottles) about every two hours in the early months. Bottle-feeding can be done by the father, other family members, and trusted caregivers. This option leaves the mother free to do other things, such as go to school or work.

Taking Care of Yourself

Your first few months at home with your baby will require a lot of adjustment. You may feel sad and lonely for the first few weeks after giving birth. Your emotions may swing for no reason. This is normal; your hormones are still in flux. Some women begin to feel a deep sadness, lack of energy, negative thoughts, and sense of despair. This is called postpartum depression and is not at all unusual. You should speak to your doctor about it. He or she may prescribe medicine that will help you until your body chemistry settles down and returns to normal. The doctor may also recommend that you get counseling to help you with this transition.

Having family and friends to keep you company is a great help during the first few months of being a mother. If you have

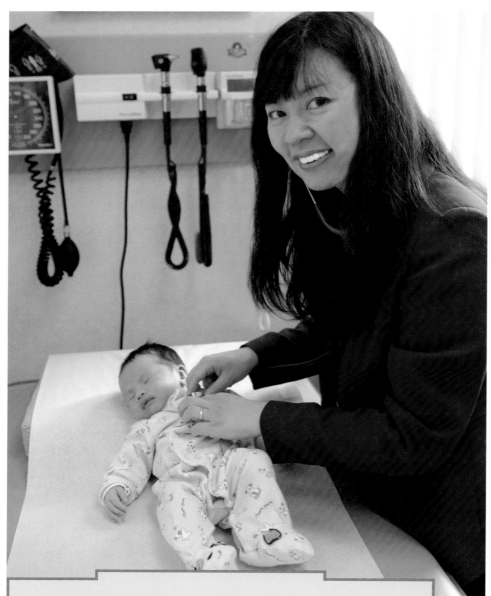

A pediatrician examines a newborn. You will need to be attentive to your baby's care and visit your doctor as often as he or she recommends.

the love and support of others, you will feel less worried and less alone. Getting out of the house once in a while is also important. Sometimes you may want to take your baby for a walk or to the park. Other times, you may want to leave the baby with a trusted person so you can have some time on your own. Having some personal time can keep you from feeling trapped and frustrated by motherhood. It reminds you that, even though you have a baby, you can also still have some time that is yours alone. You're still an individual, defined by your personality and interests, not just by motherhood.

Glossary

abortion The process of ending a pregnancy.

abstinence Choosing not to have sex.

acquired immunodeficiency syndrome (AIDS) A fatal sexually transmitted disease that attacks the body's immune system.

adoption The procedure through which a baby or child is given up by the biological parents to be raised by adoptive parents.

anemia A deficiency of red blood cells that makes a person feel weak and tired all the time.

arteries The vessels that carry blood from the heart to the body.

contraception Methods of prevention of conception and pregnancy; birth control.

embryo The term for the fertilized egg during the first two months of pregnancy.

fallopian tubes Tubes near the ovaries where the egg is fertilized.

fetus The term for the embryo after three months.

hormones Chemicals in the body that stimulate growth or change.

Lamaze A method of childbirth that involves exercises and breathing control to give pain relief without medications.

menstruation The monthly loss of blood and other matter from the uterus.

ovaries Female sex glands that hold a female's eggs.

ovulation The release of a mature egg.

ovum A mature egg.

pediatricians Doctors who specialize in the care of children.

placenta Vitamin-rich organ that joins the fetus to the mother's uterus during pregnancy and nourishes it.

postpartum depression A mood disorder, where a mother feels severe sadness or depression after childbirth.

premature Not yet fully developed; in an early stage of development.

prenatal Before birth.

puberty A time of growth, change, and sexual maturity early in the teenage years.

sonogram An image of the fetus inside the uterus made by a machine using sound waves.

sperm The male fertilizing cell or "seed."

uterus The organ in which a fetus develops; also called the womb.

The Adoption Council of Canada (ACC)
211 Bronson Avenue
Ottawa, ON K1R 6H5
Canada
(613) 235-0344
Web site: http://www.adoption.ca
The Adoption Council of Canada (ACC) is the umbrella
  organization for adoption in Canada.

American Adoption Congress (AAC)
Web site: http://www.americanadoptioncongress.org
This organization is committed to adoption reform and to
  making the public aware of the realities of adopted life
  for both birth and adoptive families.

America's Pregnancy Helpline
(888) 672-2296
Web site: http://www.thehelpline.org
America's Pregnancy Helpline is a national health organization committed to ongoing reproductive research
  and education.

National Campaign to Prevent Teen Pregnancy
1776 Massachusetts Avenue NW, Suite 200

Washington, DC 20036

(202) 478-8500

Web site: http://www.teenpregnancy.org

The National Campaign to Prevent Teen Pregnancy is a non-
profit initiative whose mission is to improve the well-being
of children, youth, and families by reducing teen pregnancy.

National Women's Health Network

514 10th Street NW, Suite 400

Washington, DC 20005

(202) 347-1140

Web site: http://www.nwhn.org

The National Women's Health Network improves the health of
all women by developing and promoting a critical analysis
of health issues in order to affect policy and support consumer decision making.

Parenting Questions and Answers

Web site: http://www.parenting-qa.com

Parenting-QA.com provides a resource for parents to get
help with many of the questions that will arise when
raising children.

Planned Parenthood Federation of America

434 West 33rd Street

New York, NY 10001

(800) 230-PLAN (7526)

Web site: http://www.ppfa.org

Planned Parenthood provides comprehensive reproductive and
related health care services in settings that preserve and
protect the privacy and rights of each individual.

Toronto Health Connection
(416) 338-7600
Web site: http://www.toronto.ca/health/thc_index.htm
Toronto Public Health maintains Toronto Health Connection,
and works to provide services that protect Canadians'
overall health.

Women, Infants, and Children (WIC) Program
Web site: http://www.fns.usda.gov/wic
WIC helps safeguard the health of low-income women
and children (up to age five). The WIC Web site is main-
tained by the Food and Nutrition Service. Each U.S. state
has a toll-free number for respective state agencies for
contacting a WIC in your area. Check out http://www.
fns.usda.gov/wic/Contacts/tollfreenumbers.htm.

Web Sites

Due to the changing nature of Internet links, Rosen Publishing
has developed an online list of Web sites related to the subject
of this book. This site is updated regularly. Please use this link
to access the list:

http://www.rosenlinks.com/faq/preg

Ehrlich, J. Shoshanna. *Who Decides? The Abortion Rights of Teens*. New York, NY: Praeger Publications, 2006.

Feinstein, Stephen. *Sexuality and Teens: What You Should Know About Sex, Abstinence, Birth Control, Pregnancy, and STDs*. Berkeley Heights, NJ: Enslow Publishers, 2009.

Frohnapfel-Krueger, Lisa. *Teen Pregnancy and Parenting* (Current Controversies). Farmington Hills, MI: Greenhaven Press, 2010.

Gaudette, Pat. *Teen Mom: A Journal*. Lecanto, FL: Home & Leisure Publishing, 2008.

Howard-Barr, Elissa, and Stacey M. Barrineau. *The Truth About Sexual Behavior and Unplanned Pregnancy*. New York, NY: Facts On File, 2009.

Hyde, Margaret, and Elizabeth Forsyth. *Safe Sex 101: An Overview for Teens*. New York, NY: Twenty-First Century Books, 2006.

Lindsay, Jeanne Warren. *Teen Dads: Rights, Responsibilities & Joys* (Teen Pregnancy and Parenting). Cerrito, CA: Morning Glory Press, 2008.

Roles, Patricia. *Facing Teenage Pregnancy: A Handbook for the Pregnant Teen*. Washington, DC: Child Welfare League of America, 2006.

Williams, Heidi. *Teen Pregnancy* (Issues That Concern You). Farmington Hills, MI: Greenhaven Press, 2009.

Index

About the Authors

Carol P. Campbell is a paraprofessional in public education and a writer who lives in Michigan.

Tamra Orr has a degree in English and education from Ball State University. She lives in the Pacific Northwest and is the mother of four children. She is the author of numerous non-fiction books for people of all ages, including such topics as cancer, date rape, personal strength and self acceptance for teen girls, and public health research.

Photo Credits

Cover © www.istockphoto.com/Olivier Lantzendörffer; p. 5 KRT/Newscom; pp. 7, 9, 51 Shutterstock.com; p. 13 Bloomberg via Getty Images; p. 15 © John Powell Photographer/Alamy; pp. 18, 35 Comstock/Thinkstock; p. 22 © Steve Skjold/Alamy; p. 25 BananaStock/Thinkstock; p. 28 Tina Stallard/Getty Images; pp. 31, 54 New York Daily News via Getty Images; p. 33 © Angela Hampton Picture Library/Alamy; p. 39 © www.istockphoto.com/David Sucsy; p. 47 © AP Images; p. 52 Jupiterimages/Creatas/Thinkstock.

Designer: Evelyn Horovicz; Editor: Kathy Kuhtz Campbell; Photo Researcher: Peter Tomlinson